KARATE
techniques & tactics

Pierre Blot

Foreword by J. Allen Queen

Sterling Publishing Co., Inc. New York

A big thank-you to the children of the Karate Club of Suresnes for their help on this book.

Photo Credits

All photographs by René Fonsart, except for those on pages 6, 13, 23, 25, 27, 79, 104, 136, 140, and 141, which were provided by Presse-Sports Agency

Edited by Claire Bazinet
Translated by Marguerite Gregory

10 9 8 7 6 5 4 3 2 1

This edition published in 2002 by
Sterling Publishing Company, Inc.
387 Park Avenue South, New York, N.Y. 10016
First published by Editions MILAN, 300 rue Léon-Joulin,
31101 Toulouse Cedex 01 France
© 1993 by Editions MILAN
English translation © 1996 by Sterling Publishing Co., Inc.
previously published under the title *Karate for Beginners*
Distributed in Canada by Sterling Publishing
c/o Canadian Manda Group, One Atlantic Avenue, Suite 105,
Toronto, Ontario, Canada M6K 3E7
Distributed in Great Britain and Europe by Chris Lloyd at Orca Book
Services, Stanley House, Fleets Lane, Poole BH15 3AJ, England.
Distributed in Australia by Capricorn Link (Australia) Pty. Ltd.
P.O. Box 704, Windsor, NSW 2756 Australia

Printed in China
All rights reserved

Sterling ISBN 0-8069-8217-9

Contents

Foreword

As a karate student and teacher for thirty years, I am pleased to endorse a quality book with such excellent detail and quality instruction as Blot's *Karate for Beginners*. Pierre Blot is well known in the world of martial arts and has won several karate championships. Many of his students have performed well in challenging karate competition, winning several championships at their respective levels.

Blot is a master of the major Japanese style of karate known as Shotokan and has been instrumental in promoting the Shotokan style throughout the world. In his book, he has been successful in presenting the basic karate skills of the great masters in an easy-to-read, colorful format. His stimulating teaching techniques, captured in book form, are now available to enlighten and inspire those eager to begin an exciting adventure learning the ancient art of karate.

—Professor J. Allen Queen, Black Belt Fifth Degree
Author of several popular karate books, including
Karate Basics, Complete Karate and *Karate for Kids*

Pierre Blot, black belt fifth dan Shotokan, ex-champion of Europe, three-time French champion, member of the *Equipe de France*, karate instructor, and technical adviser.

Starting Karate

You may be shy and lack self-confidence. You may have a hard time making friends. The practice of karate will help you overcome these difficulties through group training and through your own individual work.

You may be nervous or need to channel your aggressiveness. You may have been told you are a bad sport. Karate will teach you self-control through healthy competition. The karate way of life awaits you.

This book will familiarize you with karate in a simple and effective way. You begin by learning the basic movements that will enable you to rise from one rank to the next on the way to your black belt. You learn about competition and the rules of arbitration. You also meet here some great champions past and present—and who knows but, perhaps someday, you may be among the champions of tomorrow.

When you talk with your friends, tell them about karate, a discipline so often unappreciated and misunderstood. Encourage their interest and maybe they will practise it, too. And never forget that karate has always been and is, first and foremost, an art—and then a sport.

Good luck and good training!

At what age should you begin?

Most clubs accept children who have reached the age of six or seven. Starting earlier is not recommended because of the level of concentration that the discipline requires of the karateka, or student. Practicing karate at a young age will enable you to gain a sound knowledge of your body and develop good coordination.

The quality of the instruction

Once you have decided to study karate, it is important to get a good start. Any bad habits you may develop will take much time and effort to correct, so you must choose your instructor carefully. Gather as much information as you can on the club of your choice as well as on the karate instructor. Ask about the instructor's personal experience and qualifications. Has the instructor ever trained black belts? Is he or she used to dealing with children?

What you will wear (your karategi)

The basic uniform, or karategi, is usually white and consists of a pair of pants and a loose jacket tied at the waist with a belt. You are expected to treat your "gi" with respect. It should be kept clean at all times and folded carefully after each training session. It should fit comfortably and not get in the way when you move.

The belt you wear as part of your uniform will be a different color as you increase in grade, or kyu. A karategi that fits well gives the karateka a good image.

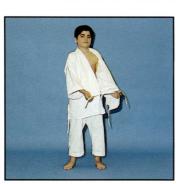

Folding your karategi

The training hall (dojo)

Traditionally, a karate dojo has a wooden floor; some clubs, however, where other martial arts such as judo and aikido are practised, may have matted floors. The walls of the dojo are covered with mirrors. These are very important because they enable you to see and so correct faults in your stance and technique. You will also see, hanging in a place of honor on the wall of every dojo, a likeness of the master of the school.

Adjoining the dojo is a locker room with showers. This is where you change before and after class and mingle with the other students. Once you enter the dojo, discipline must prevail.

What happens in class?

A karate class lasts one to two hours. It starts with bows of respect. Your first bow will be to show respect to the master of the school, whose portrait is generally hung on the wall. Next, you bow to your instructor.

You begin the class by doing warm-up exercises that prepare your muscles and joints for the workout.

You also practise balancing, which is essential in karate.

When you are ready, your instructor will demonstrate a technique. You will then execute it along with the instructor, and then alone. The instructor will watch and offer personal assistance to help each student correct his or her mistakes. The same techniques will be demonstrated many times over, with the instructor giving added help and guidance as needed. At the end of the class, the instructor will ask if everyone understands all that has been taught. This is your opportunity to communicate with your instructor. The instructor is there to help you progress.

Respect for tradition

The discipline of karate was developed by Chinese and Japanese masters. It is important to respect its traditions. They will help you understand how the discipline evolved up to today and will continue to progress into the future. Respecting the karate tradition includes taking proper care of your gi, practising good hygiene, showing respect to other students, to your instructor and your dojo, and paying homage to the master of the school before and after each class. After a while, the values instilled by the practice of karate will become part of your everyday life.

Talking with the instructor

Karate can help you blossom, especially if you are in harmony with your instructor. You will have someone you can talk to about karate and its traditions, and also about other things in your life, such as your interactions with other karatekas, school friends, teachers, and your parents. Your karate instructor should be a person you can confide in because of the profound respect on which your relationship is based.

Belt rank and promotion

Depending on your karate school, there may be more grades or different belt colors. Also, promotions in rank may be awarded in different ways:

1 Based on kyu grades, from the white belt class through to the brown belt.
2 By completing training associated with the different belt colors, each one corresponding to a kyu.

At black belt level, the rankings are referred to as degrees, or dans.

	KYU	BELT	
6	Sixth		White
5	Fifth		Yellow
4	Fourth		Orange
3	Third		Green
2	Second		Blue
1	First		Brown
			Black

Advances in grades are often awarded by the student's instructor, until the student reaches the highest or first kyu. In some schools, black belts and degrees may be given to a student by an instructor who has reached the status of karate master; elsewhere, promotion at this higher level is only awarded by a panel of judges, who evaluate the student's performance.

Belt-rank tests take place in three stages:

1 Performing the fundamental techniques (kion)
2 Sparring (gohon kumite, sambon kumite, ippon kumite, jyu ippon kumite)
3 Katas (the performance of a sequence of techniques relevant to the current rank).

This method of promotion applies to all belt rank promotions up to the level of black belt.

Often used terms

Itch:	one
Ni:	two
Sam:	three
Tchi:	four
Go:	five
Roku:	six
Itchi:	seven
Atchi:	eight
Kou:	nine
Dijou:	ten
Ge:	low
Gohon kumite:	five-step sparring
Hadjime:	start
Hikite:	fist retracts to hip while the other punches out
Ippon kumite:	one-step sparring
Jo:	high
Kamae:	assume a ready stance
Keage:	snap
Kekomi:	thrust
Kiai:	union of breath and voice; moment of maximum release of power
Kime:	focus
Kion:	repetition of fundamental techniques
Ma:	distance
Mawate:	turn; about-face
Mokutso:	meditation
Sambon kumite:	three-step sparring
Seiza:	kneeling position
Shu:	middle
Tori:	attacker
Uke:	defender
Yame:	stop
Yoi:	waiting or ready position

Yellow Belt

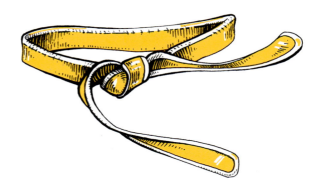

All that you have learned about karate appeals to you. The precise and powerful techniques you have seen demonstrated by experienced karatekas or champions appear simple enough. However, it is important to remember that karate is a discipline that requires patience and perseverance. You, too, can be successful if you will take the time to learn. You already know what to wear, how to tie your belt, and what is expected of you. Now you must earn your first colored belt. This first program will help you reach your goal.

The techniques

THE BOWS
  Ritsurei
  Zarei
DACHI
  Hachigi dachi
  Zen kutsu dachi
  Ko kutsu dachi
TSUKI WASA
  Choku tsuki
  Oi tsuki
  Striking points
  Gyaku tsuki
  Sambon tsuki
UKE WASA
  Gedan barai
  Soto uke
  Age uke
  Shuto uke
GOHON KUMITE
MAWATE
KERI WASA
  Mae geri
  Striking points
THE KATAS
  Taikyoku shodan
  Heian shodan

The Warm-up

Preparing your body for the workout before attempting any of the special karate techniques is very important and indispensable.

The warm-up should take about ten minutes. The exercises will help you to focus yourself mentally for the workout to follow and to concentrate better on the techniques as well as to avoid injury.

During the ten-minute warm-up, do exercises to loosen up your joints and stretch your muscles in order to prepare them for the training session.

The Bows

The bow is a sign of mutual respect between opponents, and between karatekas and their instructor. It is also a sign of respect towards your school. Every exercise begins and ends with a bow.

Ritsurei (STANDING BOW)

1 Yoi position.

2 Move and lock the right foot (misubi dachi position).

3 Bend upper body forward.

4 Return to upright position.

5 Move right foot to side (yoi position).

Zarei (KNEELING BOW)

1 Heels together, arms at sides (misubi dachi position).

2 Kneel by placing left knee on floor.

3 Place right knee on floor, sit on crossed feet.

4 Put left hand down on the floor.

5 Position right hand touching left hand.

6 Lean forward, head reaching towards hands.

7 Return to upright position.

8 Place right hand on right thigh.

9 Place left hand on left thigh.

10 Feet flat and crossed.

Dachi

Hachigi dachi
(YOI STANCE)

The yoi position, or hachigi dachi, is the alert stance assumed while waiting or preparing for an exercise, such as kata, kion, ippon kumite.

1 Arms at sides, feet together (heisoku dachi position).

2 Cross the two arms.

3 Step the right foot to the side as you uncross the arms.

Zen kutsu dachi
(FRONT STANCE)

You will assume this basic stance often during karate training. It is generally used when preparing to attack. About 70% of the body weight is placed on the front leg and 30% on the leg extended rearward. The position of the feet is double shoulder width from front to rear and a shoulder

1 Hands on hips, feet spread apart.

Ko kutsu dachi
(BACK STANCE)

This is another basic stance. It is used for defensive techniques. About 70% of the body weight is placed on the back leg and 30% on the front leg, which is slightly bent. The stance is double shoulder width from front to back. The front foot forms a 90°

1 Hands on hips, feet together.

2 Move right leg forward and bend at knee. Back leg is extended. Hips face forward.

3 Step forward into middle position with feet together. Legs are bent.

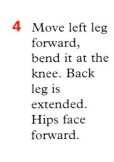

4 Move left leg forward, bend it at the knee. Back leg is extended. Hips face forward.

5 Feet are hip-width apart. Place 70% of body weight on front leg.

width from left to right. The front knee bends forward to a position just above the toes and aligned with the foot. The back foot should be turned as much as possible in the same direction, depending on the flexibility of the ankle.

Important: Both feet remain flat on the floor. The chest must be perpendicular to the floor, not leaning forward.

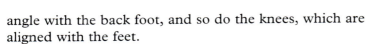

2 Open right foot to 90° angle. Bend legs.

3 Move left leg forward, on a line with right heel.

4 Move right leg forward into middle position. Feet together, legs bent.

5 Point left foot at 90° angle. Legs bent.

6 Move right leg forward, on a line with left heel. Place 70% of body weight on back leg. Both heels are aligned.

angle with the back foot, and so do the knees, which are aligned with the feet.

Important: Both feet should remain flat on the floor and the chest perpendicular to the floor.

Tsuki Wasa

Choku tsuki
(STRAIGHT PUNCH)

IN PLACE

1 Hachigi dachi with left arm extended, right fist at hip.

2 Punch out with right fist at the same time as left fist is drawn back. Keep elbows close to body.

3 Complete movement by rotating both fists.

IN MOTION

4 Move left leg forward into zen kutsu dachi. Left arm extended, right fist at hip.

5 Move right leg forward into middle position. Right fist punches out as left arm is retracted. Hips remain level.

6 Complete zen kutzu arm action with rotation of both fists. Hips and shoulders face forward.

Oi tsuki
(LUNGE PUNCH)

This punching technique is executed while stepping forward. As you advance your right leg, you punch with your right fist. You punch out as your foot is set down and retract your other fist to your hip at the same time. Repeating this exercise allows you to throw multiple, succeeding punches.

Important: The entire movement must be executed in perfect balance for maximum effectiveness of the oi tsuki technique.

Striking Surfaces

Making a fist

a Hand is open

b Curl up fingers

c Lock thumb over fingers to make fist (seiken)

1 Uraken

2 Seiken
2 also Tettsui (*see* **12**)

3 Nukite .

4 Haito

5 Ippon nukite

6 Nihon nukite

24

Tsuki Wasa

Striking Surfaces

7 Uraken

8 Makadaka ken

9 Haishu

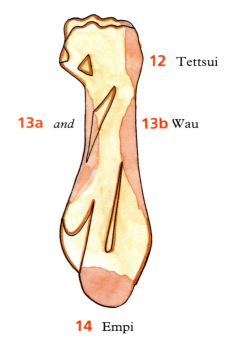

12 Tettsui

13a *and* **13b** Wau

10 Shuto

11 Teisho

14 Empi

Gyaku tsuki
(REVERSE PUNCH)

This technique is executed with the reverse fist; in other words if your left foot is forward, your right fist will punch out. You can use this technique from a stationary position or while moving.

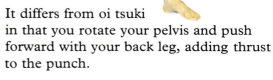

It differs from oi tsuki in that you rotate your pelvis and push forward with your back leg, adding thrust to the punch.

Important: Your shoulders should *not* rotate with the pelvis but remain facing forward. Gyaku tsuki is a very powerful technique used primarily to counterattack.

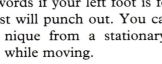

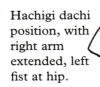

1 Hachigi dachi position, with right arm extended, left fist at hip.

2 Move right leg forward into middle position.

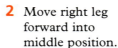

3 Move into a zen kutsu stance. Hips at 45° angle, but shoulders face forward.

4 Thrust left hip forward and, at same time, extend left arm while rotating both fists. Hips face forward and pelvis is level.

Uke Wasa

Gedan barai
(DOWNWARD BLOCK)

With a sweeping outward motion, the forearm deflects any attack to the abdomen. The movement begins with the fist in position near the ear, palm facing in. The blocking arm swings down along the outstretched arm while the hips rotate to a 45° angle. As the blocking arm reaches its end position above the knee, the other arm is drawn back to the hip.

Important: The striking surface is located between the wrist and the elbow on the forearm.

IN PLACE

1 Hachigi dachi position. Bring left fist up to right ear. Right arm is extended. Hips face forward.

2 Slide left arm down along the right while rotating hips at a 45° angle. The shoulders are down.

3 End the movement by rotating both fists. Hips are at a 45° angle.

IN MOTION

6 Extend left arm over the knee. Retract right fist to the hip. Hips at a 45° angle. Shoulders down.

5 Move left leg forward into zen kutsu. Hips face forward.

7 Move right leg forward into middle position. Bring right fist up to the left ear. Hips facing forward. Pelvis remains level.

Middle position of Gedan barai: left arm slides down along right arm.

4 Hachigi dachi position. Arms are in ready position.

8 Complete the downward block by stepping into a right zen kutsu stance. Hips at a 45° angle. Rotate both fists.

29

Gohon kumite
(FIVE-STEP SPARRING)

This is a sparring movement for two opponents. After bowing to your partner, you execute a series of five attacks which is countered by five blocks. The exercise is preset. Both karatekas know the attacks and blocks to be executed, so can fully concentrate on their moves.

The exercise begins with the partners face to face, the attacker in a zen kutsu stance and the defender in a normal waiting stance and ready to block. The attacker steps forward, executing the pre-arranged technique. The defender steps back into a zen kutsu stance and blocks accordingly. Unless the instructor calls for it, the only counterattack allowed is a kiai on completing the fifth step.

Important: After the fifth step, you will bow to one another and reverse roles. Try not to lose your stance during the exercise. Maintaining a stable position will enable you to attack and block more effectively.

In place: Counterattack (gyaku tsuki)

Soto uke (OUTSIDE MIDDLE BLOCK)

This block will help you protect your chest as well as your face. It is a sweeping inward movement that enables you to block perpendicularly all attacks directed at your middle and upper body.

Important: As the move is completed, the blocking arm should be turned to face *you*. This is done by rotating the fist inward.

IN PLACE

1 Hachigi dachi position. The arm is out at a 90° angle, fist facing out. Hips face forward. Left arm is extended.

2 Rotate hips at a 45° angle. Shoulders are down.

3 Swing right arm across the chest and draw left fist back to the hip while rotating both fists. Hips are at a 45° angle.

32

IN MOTION

5 Move left leg in a zen kutsu stance. Hips face forward. Shoulders are down.

4 Hachigi dachi position. Left arm in ready position, right arm extended.

8 Complete block by stepping into a right zen kutsu stance. Hips are at a 45° angle. Rotate both fists.

7 Move right leg forward into middle position. Right arm is in ready position. Hips face forward. The pelvis remains level.

6 Swing left arm in front of the chest and draw right fist back to the hip while rotating both fists. Hips at a 45° angle.

Gohon kumite
(FIVE-STEP SPARRING)

In place: Counterattack (gyaku tsuki)

Age uke

(UPWARD BLOCK)

This defense technique will help you protect your face from blows coming from the left or the right, whether you are moving forward or backward. The goal is to deflect all attacks directed at the face upward. The age uke, like all other blocks, is done with the hips at a 45° angle in order to use the forward thrust of the hips to deliver a counterattack.

Important: The elbow should be slightly lower than the fist to lessen the trauma of the impact on the arm.

IN PLACE

1 Hachigi dachi. Right fist at hip, left arm extended.

2 Bring right arm underneath the left. Hips at a 45° angle. Shoulders down.

3 Swing right arm straight up and bring left fist back to the hip. Hips at a 45° angle.

36

IN MOTION

6 Bring left arm underneath your right. Hips facing forward.

5 Move left leg forward into a zen kutsu stance. Hips face forward. Shoulders are down.

4 Hachigi dachi. Right arm extended, left fist at hip.

8 Move right leg forward into middle position. Start raising your right arm. Hips face forward.

9 Complete zen kutsu stance while raising your right arm in front of the face. Hips at a 45° angle. Rotate both fists.

7 Raise left arm in front of your face while drawing right fist back to the hip. Hips are at a 45° angle. Rotate both fists.

37

Gohon kumite
(FIVE-STEP SPARRING)

In place: Counterattack (gyaku tsuki)

Shuto uke (KNIFEHAND BLOCK)

Shuto uke is an outward block, which can also be used to strike as with many other techniques of this type. Its purpose is to protect the chest and the face. The technique is executed with the hand open and flat and the fingers pressed together. The blocking hand starts out near the ear and ends with the palm facing outward and on a line with the forearm and shoulder. The edge of the hand is the striking surface. The other arm, which is at first extended forwards, is drawn back to the solar plexus, or abdomen. The pelvis, at the same time, tilts backwards.

Important: You must complete the technique with the foot, the knee, the hand, the forearm, the elbow, and the shoulder *aligned*; and the hips at a 45° angle.

IN PLACE

1 Hachigi dachi position. Ready position with left hand at right ear. Right arm extended.

2 Hips at a 45° angle. Shoulders down.

3 Swing left hand down across the chest and draw right hand back above the belt. Hips at a 45° angle. Left arm bent at a 90° angle.

APPLICATION

8 Complete ko kutsu dachi. Bring right hand down across the chest and draw left hand back above the belt. Hips at a 45° angle. Rotate both hands.

7 Move right leg forward into middle position. Right hand in ready position at left ear with left arm extended. Hips facing forward. Shoulders down.

IN MOTION

4 Hachigi dachi. Ready position with left hand at right ear. Right arm extended.

5 Slide your right foot out at a 90° angle while bending both legs. Hips at a 45° angle.

6 Move left leg forward into ko kutsu dachi. Bring left hand down across the chest and draw right hand back above the belt. Left arm bent at a 90° angle. Rotate both hands.

Gohon kumite
(FIVE-STEP SPARRING)

In place: Counterattack (gyaku tsuki)

Mawate

Karate exercises are generally performed in a continuing and rhythmical pattern. To avoid breaks in the sequences, the about-face, or half-turn, technique known as mawate is used. It enables you to reposition yourself in the opposite direction in the same ready stance. These half turns are commonly used in katas.

Technique A

1 Right zen kutsu stance.

2 Bring right foot next to left foot.

3 Extend right leg back diagonally.

4 Pivot on both feet. Zen kutsu dachi.

Technique B

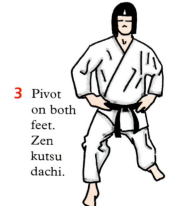

1 Left zen kutsu dachi.

2 Extend right leg back and to the side.

3 Pivot on both feet. Zen kutsu dachi.

Tsuki Wasa

Sambon tsuki (TRIPLE PUNCH)

This technique is a combination of the oi tsuki, gyaku tsuki, and tsuki techniques. It is a one-step combination. The three punches can be directed at different levels.

Important: It is imperative to deliver each punch with the *same thrust*. The speed of execution will depend on how swiftly the fist is drawn back to the hip.

1 Right zen kutsu dachi. Right tsuki to the face.

2 In place. Giyaku tsuki to the chest.

3 In place. Tsuki to the belt.

Keri Wasa

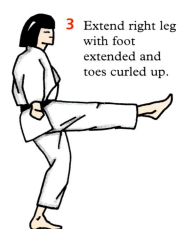

Mae geri (FRONT KICK)

Mae geri is a very powerful forward kick, directed at a target straight ahead of you. The foot is extended and the toes are curled (koshi). After the kick, the leg is retracted, bending at the knee, and is ready to kick out again. There are two variations on this technique: the front snap kick (keage), in which the leg is immediately withdrawn to its original position, and the front thrust kick (kekomi), in which the leg remains extended longer to maximize the impact on the target.

Important: Balance is achieved by bending the supporting leg slightly and contracting the abdominal muscles. The shoulders should be relaxed.

IN MOTION

1 Zen kutsu dachi position. Arms at sides.

2 Raise right knee to the belt. Hips face forward. Left leg is slightly bent.

3 Extend right leg with foot extended and toes curled up.

4 Bring right leg back to bent position.

46

5 Set leg down in zen kutsu dachi.

6 Raise left knee. Pelvis remains level.

7 Extend left leg.

9 Set leg down in a zen kutsu stance.

8 Bring left leg back to bent position.

47

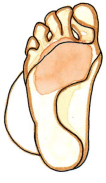

14

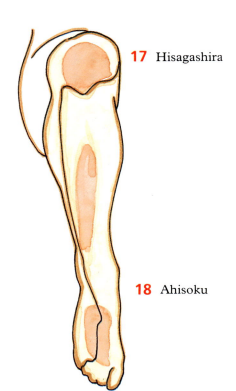

17 Hisagashira

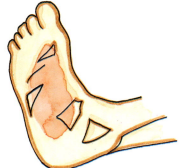

15 Teisoku

16 Kakato

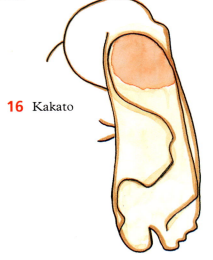

18 Ahisoku

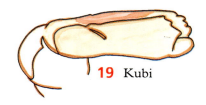

19 Kubi

48

THE KATAS

Katas are the bedrock of karate. They are fundamental to the development of proper technique. Katas consist of a combination of movements that are performed alone according to a set pattern. Every attack and every block has a specific purpose. They are part of an imaginary combat against several opponents. Repeated practise of katas will enable you to develop greater concentration, balance, and speed of execution.

Important: When performing a kata, you must never look down but always straight ahead at your imaginary opponent. This will help you to focus and to execute your kata with sincerity. A powerless and unconvincing kata is a lifeless kata.

You will learn your katas, technique by technique, slowly, respecting the set pattern. Execute each movement carefully and avoid losing your balance. Once you have memorized your kata, you can then add power and rhythm to it. Certain movements are done in combination, others individually. Some are executed in slow motion and some are combined with a kiai. A good instructor will be able to judge your proficiency in karate by the way in which you execute a basic kata. Katas can be performed at different speeds and are an excellent warm-up exercise.

Important: You will notice that katas always begin with a defense technique, since defense is the main purpose of karate.

The katas presented in this book are limited to the basic katas. You will learn the more advanced forms with your instructor.

Taikyoku shodan kata

In all, there are six taikyoku katas. The pattern and techniques are very basic and consist of two or three movements repeated throughout the form. The repetition enables you to keep a clear mind and to concentrate on the balance of each stance and on the power of your blocks and counterattacks. Each taikyoku consists of twenty movements evolving along the same set pattern. The direction of the movements and the turns remain the same. Once you have mastered the taikyoku shodan here, you will have no difficulty learning the other five.

Important: There are two powerful points in each taikyoku. They are called kiai. A kiai is a sound released with the breath. Each movement is accompanied by an in-breath or an out-breath. You breathe in as you prepare for a move, you breathe out as you execute it. The greatest power is released at the end of the out-breath as a kiai. The main difference between each taikyoku is the transition between stances and between blocks.

THE KATAS
Taikyoku shodan

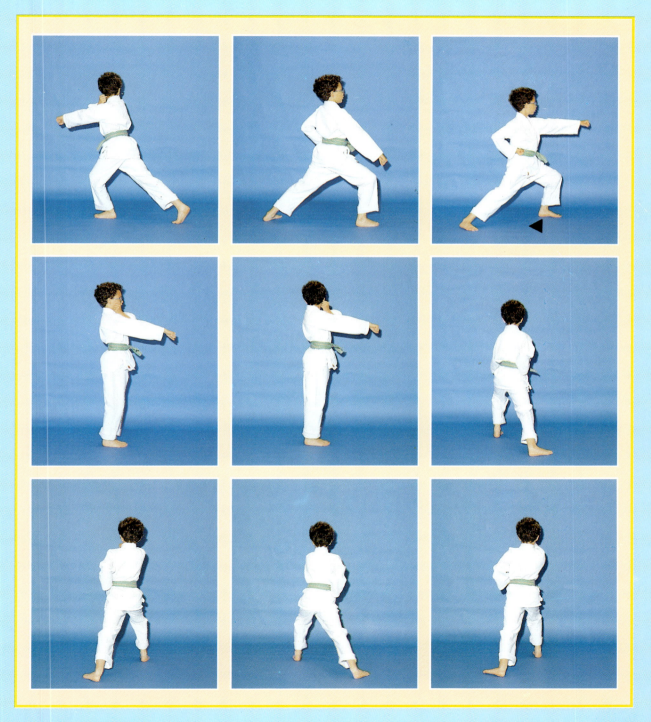

THE KATAS
Taikyoku shodan

Heian shodan kata

There are five heian katas required for promotion to black belt. Heian shodan, the first, consists mainly of blocks and counterattacks in zen kutsu. The last four movements are executed in ko kutsu.

Important: Intermediate positions are the same as in taikyoku shodan kata.

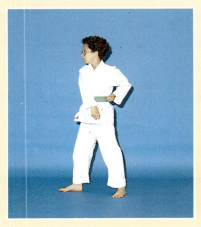

Orange Belt

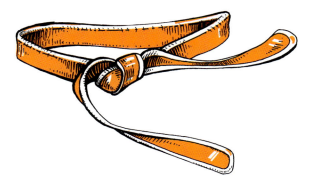

If you have completed training and received your yellow belt from your instructor, congratulations! You are now ready to start the orange belt program. This training will be much easier since all the new techniques which you are about to learn apply the basic stances, which you already know.

This is the kyu in which you will learn the most techniques. You need to learn to do them smoothly and master them as you advance in rank. Sparring will now become a three-step exercise (*sambon kumite*).

The techniques

DACHI
Neko ashi dachi
Kiba dachi
Shiko dachi

TSUKI WASA
Age empi uchi
Mawashi empi uchi
Yoko empi uchi
Otoshi empi uchi
Ushiro empi uchi
Shuto uchi
Soto shuto uchi
Soto tettsui uchi
Tettsui uchi — Uraken

UKE WASA
Uchi uke
Sambon kumite
(application)
Morote uke

KERI WASA
Mikazuki geri
Mawashi geri

THE KATAS
Heian nidan

59

Dachi

Neko ashi dachi
(CAT STANCE)

Neko ashi dachi, also known as the cat stance, is a waiting stance usually used on defense. This stance lacks mobility, as most of the body weight rests on the back leg.

1 Hands on hips. Feet together.

2 Slide right foot out at 90°. Legs are bent.

3 Move left foot forward slightly and in line with right heel. Lift left heel; 90% of body weight rests on back leg.

4 Move right foot forward into middle position.

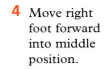

7 Most of body weight (90%) rests on back leg. Both heels are aligned. Hips face forward.

5 Slide left foot out at a 90° angle. Legs bent.

6 Move right foot slightly forward, in line with left heel. Lift right heel.

Kiba dachi (HORSE STANCE)

This stance, with legs spread wide apart, is called the horse stance. Because the body weight is distributed evenly over both legs, the stance is very stable. Kiba dachi is mostly used for side attacks.

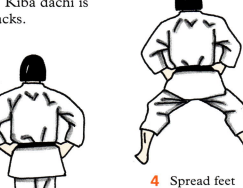

4 Spread feet apart to double hip width by moving right foot out. Feet are parallel. Body weight rests evenly on both legs.

3 Move right foot and turn on left. Feet together. Legs bent.

2 Spread feet to double hip width by moving left foot out to side. Feet are parallel. Body weight rests evenly on both legs.

1 Feet together. Legs bent.

Shiko dachi

A variation on the kiba dachi position. Here, feet are open at a 45° angle.

61

Tsuki Wasa

Age empi uchi (UPWARD ELBOW STRIKE)

Empi uchi is a very powerful bodily weapon and dangerous if it is not used with respect and absolute control. This short-distance technique is often used in close combat. All uchi techniques require preparation, unlike oi tsuki, gyaku tsuki, etc.

IN MOTION

1 Zen kutsu dachi. Gedan barai.

2 Move right leg forward into middle position. Raise right fist to shoulder level. Pelvis remains level.

3 Complete zen kutsu dachi, raising elbow to face level. Left fist at the hip. Hips face forward.

4 Move left leg forward into middle position. Raise left fist to shoulder level. Hips face forward.

5 Complete zen kutsu dachi, raising elbow to face level. Right fist at the hip.

Mawashi empi uchi
(CIRCULAR ELBOW STRIKE)

1 Zen kutsu dachi position. Gedan barai.

2 Move right leg forward into middle position. Right elbow swings out and around. Left arm is extended.

3 Complete zen kutsu dachi. Bring right elbow around in front of the face. Hips at a 45° angle. Left fist at the hip.

Yoko empi uchi
(SIDE ELBOW STRIKE)

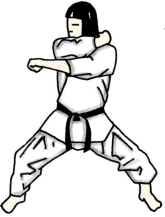

1 Kiba dachi position. Right elbow in ready position above left arm.

2 Right elbow strikes out to side, in line with the shoulder. Left fist at the hip.

63

Otoshi empi uchi
(DOWNWARD ELBOW STRIKE)

1 Kiba dachi position. Right arm extends above the head. Left arm extends straight ahead.

2 Force right elbow downward. Draw left fist back to the hip.

Ushiro empi uchi
(BACK ELBOW STRIKE)

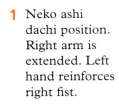

1 Neko ashi dachi position. Right arm is extended. Left hand reinforces right fist.

2 Thrust right elbow backwards, keeping it close to the body. Push with the left hand.

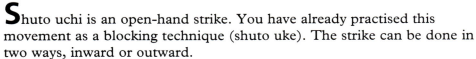

Shuto uchi
(INSIDE KNIFEHAND STRIKE)

Shuto uchi is an open-hand strike. You have already practised this movement as a blocking technique (shuto uke). The strike can be done in two ways, inward or outward.

IN MOTION

1 Hachigi dachi position. Left hand in ready position at right ear, right arm extended.

2 Set left leg down in zen kutsu dachi. Swing left hand forward and strike with edge of hand. Right fist retracts to hip. Hips at a 45° angle. Rotate both hands.

3 Move right leg forward into middle position. Right hand in ready position at left ear, left arm extended. Hips face forward. Shoulders down. Pelvis remains level.

4 Complete zen kutsu dachi. Bring right hand forward and strike with edge of hand. Hips at a 45° angle. Retract left fist to hip. Rotate both hands.

Soto shuto uchi
(OUTSIDE KNIFEHAND STRIKE)

4 Complete zen kutsu dachi. Swing right hand around in front of face. Draw left fist back to hip. Hips at a 45° angle. Rotate both hands.

IN MOTION

3 Move right leg forward into middle position. Right hand in ready position facing out, left arm extended. Hips face forward. Pelvis remains level.

2 Move left leg forward into zen kutsu dachi. Swing left hand around in front of face. Hips at a 45° angle. Draw right fist back to hip. Shoulders down. Rotate both hands.

1 Hachigi dachi. Left hand in ready position, facing out.

67

Soto tettsui uchi (OUTSIDE HAMMER STRIKE)

IN MOTION

Tettsui uchi is a hammer strike. The technique is the same as shuto uchi except that the hand is clenched, forming a tight fist. Just like shuto, it can also be used to block (uke).

1 Hachigi dachi. Left arm out in ready position at a 90° angle. Right arm is extended.

2 Set left leg down into zen kutsu dachi. Swing left arm around and strike with the side of the fist. Draw right fist back to hip.

3 Move into middle position. Right arm is held out in ready position. Left arm is extended. Hips face forward. Shoulders down.

4 Move right leg forward. Thrust right arm down and draw left fist back to the hip. Rotate both fists. Hips at a 45° angle.

Tettsui uchi (INSIDE HAMMER STRIKE)

IN MOTION

4 Move right leg further forward. Swing right arm around, striking with the side of the fist. Hips at a 45° angle.

3 Move into middle position. Right fist at left ear. Hips face forward. Left arm is extended. Shoulders down.

2 Move left leg forward into zen kutsu dachi. Strike with the side of the fist. Hips at a 45° angle. Right fist at hip.

1 Hachigi dachi. Left fist in ready position at right ear, right arm extended.

Uraken (BACKHAND STRIKE)

Uraken is similar to tettsui uchi except that the strike is done with the backhand.

IN PLACE

1 Hachigi dachi. Ready position with back of left fist facing right ear and right arm extended.

2 Start bringing the left arm around over the right arm. Hips at a 45° angle.

3 Finish movement with left arm fully extended. Draw the right fist back to the hip. Rotate both fists. Hips at a 45° angle.

DIFFERENCE IN PREPARATION

1 Ready position for uraken: Back of the hand faces the ear.

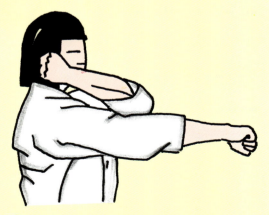

2 Ready position for gedan barai: Palm of the hand faces the ear.

IN MOTION

1 Hachigi dachi. Ready position with back of left fist facing right ear and right arm extended.

2 Move left leg forward into zen kutsu dachi. Thrust left arm out. Rotate both fists. Hips at a 45° angle. Shoulders down.

3 Move right leg forward into middle position. Pelvis remains level. Ready position, with right fist at left ear and left arm extended.

4 Complete zen kutsu dachi and thrust right arm out. Rotate both fists. Hips at a 45° angle. Draw left fist back to hip.

Uke Wasa

Uchi uke (INSIDE MIDDLE BLOCK)

Uchi uke is a basic blocking technique like gedan barai, soto uke, and jodan age uke. It is designed to protect the chest.

IN PLACE

1 Hachigi dachi. Ready position with left arm at right hip and right arm extended.

2 Rotate hips.

3 Start blocking by sliding left arm out from under the right.

4 Complete uchi uke block.

IN MOTION

4 Finish in right zen kutsu stance and block with an uchi uke. Hips at a 45° angle. Rotate both fists.

2 Move left leg forward into zen kutsu and block with an uchi uke.

3 Move into middle position while preparing for a right uchi uke block at the left hip. Hips face forward. Shoulders down.

1 Hachigi dachi. Ready position with left arm at right hip and right arm extended.

73

Sambon kumite (THREE-STEP SPARRING)

Like gohon kumite, this is an important exercise. The technique and target areas are announced, and both partners execute the movement accordingly. Unlike gohon kumite, attacks are not delivered separately but in combination, the second and third occurring in rapid succession. The third block is followed by a counterattack.

Morote uke (TWO-HAND BLOCK)

In this two-handed uchi uke, both fists are used to reinforce the block and give it more power.

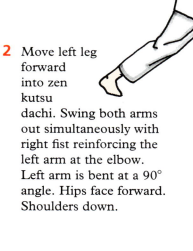

1 Hachigi dachi. Ready position with both fists at the right hip.

2 Move left leg forward into zen kutsu dachi. Swing both arms out simultaneously with right fist reinforcing the left arm at the elbow. Left arm is bent at a 90° angle. Hips face forward. Shoulders down.

Keri Wasa

Mikazuki geri

(CRESCENT KICK)

This crescent kick differs from mawashi geri in that the leg is almost fully extended. It can also be used to block. This technique can be executed two ways, towards the inside or the outside.

TO OUTSIDE FRONT VIEW

1 Left zen kutsu with arms extended down and out to the sides for balance.

2 Bring right knee up to belt level. Hips face forward.

6 Set foot down in a right zen kutsu stance.

3 Pivot on the supporting leg. Body turns sideways.

5 Return to position **2**.

4 Extend leg up and out to side to strike with the bottom of the vertical foot.

76

TO INSIDE FRONT VIEW

1 Left zen kutsu with arms extended down and out to the sides for balance.

2 Raise right knee outward to belt level. Hips face forward.

3 Extend leg up and in while pivoting on supporting leg. Strike with the arch of the vertical foot.

4 Retract knee to belt level.

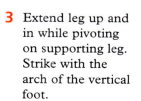

5 Set foot down in a right zen kutsu stance.

Mikazuki geri (inside)

IN MOTION

1 Right zen kutsu stance.

2 Ready position with knee at belt and foot facing inward. Hips face forward.

3 Pivot on supporting leg.

4 Extend leg up and out to strike with the instep of the vertical foot.

5 Return to position **2**.

6 Step down into a left zen kutsu stance.

Mawashi geri (ROUNDHOUSE KICK)

Mawashi geri is a circular kick that requires greater flexibility than the mae geri. You will have to exercise diligently to increase the hip opening. The pivot on the supporting leg is key to good balance and the proper placement of hip and knee for the kick. Snapping the leg back after impact is just as important as striking out, and enables you to deliver double or triple kicks.

IN PLACE

1 Hachigi dachi.

2 Raise knee to the outside, level with the belt. The supporting leg is bent.

3 Pivot on the supporting leg. Knee and foot are level.

4 Extend leg forward.

5 Back to position **2**.

IN MOTION

4 Extend leg forward.

3 Supporting leg pivots. Knee and foot are level.

2 Raise knee to the side at the level of the belt. Supporting leg is bent.

1 Zen kutsu stance.

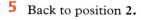

6 Set foot down in zen kutsu.

5 Back to position **2.**

THE KATAS

Heian nidan kata

Heian nidan is the second in a series of five katas. In this kata, ko kutsu is the main stance. Thirteen techniques will be executed in this position.

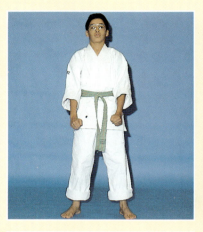

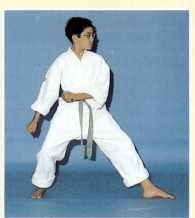

▶ same position, front view

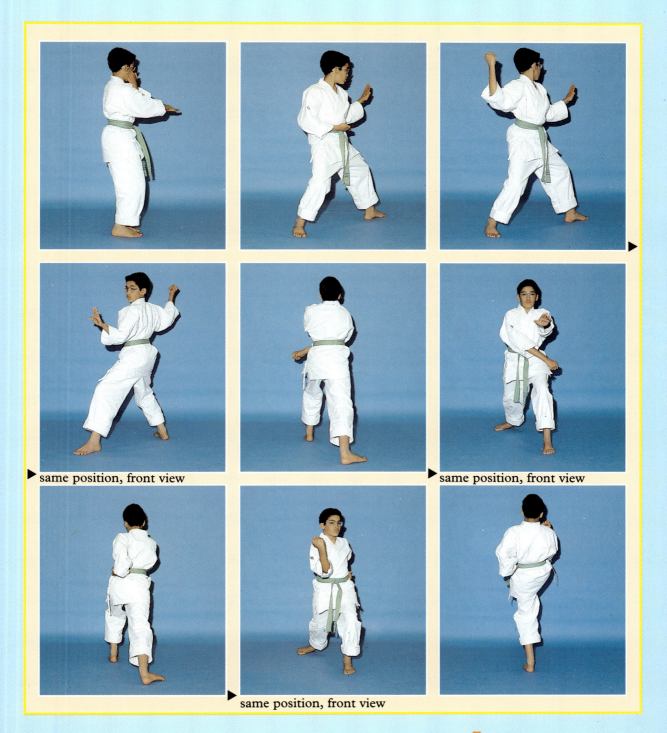

same position, front view

same position, front view

same position, front view

THE **K**ATAS
Heian nidan

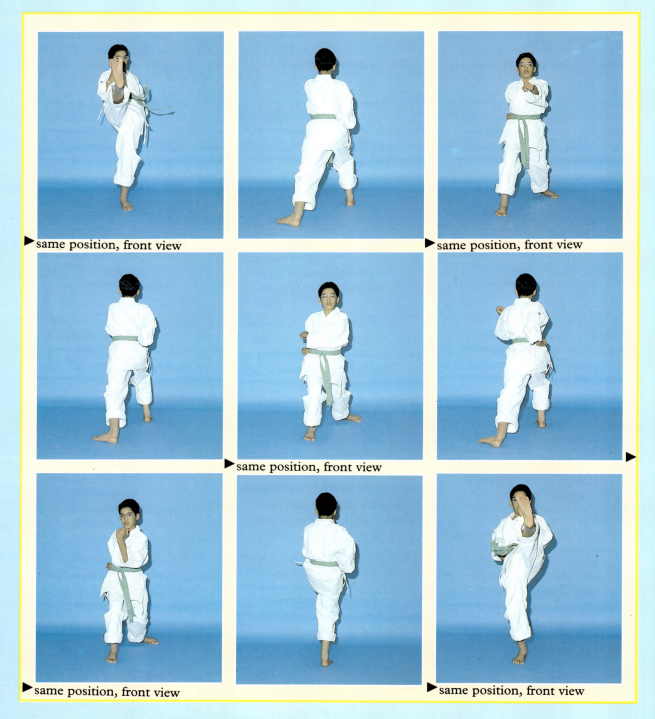

▶ same position, front view

▶ same position, front view

▶ same position, front view

▶ same position, front view

▶ same position, front view

86

▶ same position, front view

▶ same position, front view

▶ same position, front view

Green Belt

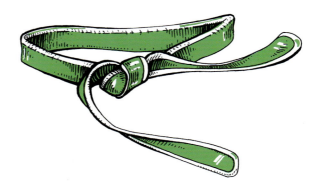

If you are ready to work towards a green belt, congratulations! What you have learned during the yellow and orange belt programs is all-important for what is to come. The green belt program brings you halfway to the black belt. The techniques and prearranged sparring you are about to learn are complex. You must be ready both physically and psychologically. So, keep up the good work.

The techniques

DACHI
    Fudo dachi
UKE WASA
    Gedan uchi barai
    Empi uke
TSUKI WASA
    Kizami tsuki
    Nukite
KERI WASA
    Yoko geri
    Ushiro geri
THE KATAS
    Heian sandan

Dachi

Fudo dachi
(IMMOVABLE STANCE)

Fudo dachi is a modification of zen kutsu. The back leg is bent so that the body weight is distributed more evenly over both legs. This stance allows for good mobility in jyu kumite (free-style sparring).

1 Zen kutsu dachi.

2 Bend back leg for fudo dachi. Hips at a 45° angle.

Uke Wasa

Gedan uchi barai
(OUTSIDE DOWNWARD BLOCK)

IN PLACE

Gedan uchi barai is a downward block that, contrary to the gedan barai, swings inward. The inside of the forearm is used as the striking surface.

1 Hachigi dachi. Ready position with right arm extended backward and palm facing up. Left arm extends forward.

2 Start bringing right arm down and around. Hips at a 45° angle. Shoulders down.

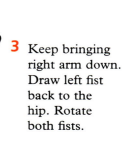

3 Keep bringing right arm down. Draw left fist back to the hip. Rotate both fists.

IN MOTION

1 Hachigi dachi. Ready position with right arm extended backward and palm facing up. Left arm extends forward.

2 Move right leg into zen kutsu dachi. Swing right arm down over the knee. Hips at a 45° angle. Rotate both fists.

3 Move left leg forward into middle position. Ready position with left arm extended backward and palm facing up. Right arm extends forward. Hips face forward. Pelvis remains level.

4 Complete zen kutsu dachi. Swing left arm down over the knee. Rotate both fists. Hips at a 45° angle.

Empi uke (ELBOW BLOCK)

Empi uke is a short elbow block. It allows you to counterattack with a quick punch. You will practise this technique in heian sandan kata.

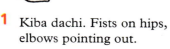

1 Kiba dachi. Fists on hips, elbows pointing out.

2 Push right elbow forward by pivoting the fist.

()

Kizami tsuki is similar to oi tsuki but with an added thrust of the hip. Rather than keeping hips forward while punching, the pelvis rotates at a 45° angle.

IN MOTION

1 Hachigi dachi. Left fist at hip and right arm extended.

2 Move left leg forward into zen kutsu. Strike out with left fist, keeping elbows close to the body. Draw right fist back to the hip. Hips at a 45° angle.

3 Move into middle position. Start retracting left fist and strike out with the right. Hips face forward. Shoulders down.

4 Move right leg all the way forward. Strike out with right fist and draw left back to the hip. Hips at a 45° angle.

Nukite (SPEARHAND STRIKE)

IN MOTION

The moves in nukite are the same as in oi tsuki except that the hand is open and the tips of the fingers are used as the striking surface. This technique is primarily directed at soft targets, such as the throat.

1 Zen kutsu dachi. Gedan barai.

2 Move right leg forward into middle position. Move open right hand forward, keeping elbows close to the body. Hips face forward. Shoulders down.

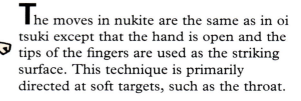

3 Complete zen kutsu dachi. Thrust right arm forward and strike with the fingertips. Hips face forward. Draw left fist back to the hip.

4 Move left leg forward into middle position. Hips face forward. Pelvis remains level. Bring left hand forward. Shoulders down.

5 Complete zen kutsu dachi. Strike with the fingertips of the left hand. Draw right fist back to the hip.

Keri Wasa

Yoko geri (SIDE KICK)

The yoko geri kick thrusts out to the side while you rotate on the supporting leg. The outer edge of the foot—from heel to toes—is used as the striking surface (sokuto).

IN PLACE

1 Hachigi dachi.

2 Raise and bend right knee at belt level, toes curled up.

3 Pivot on left foot with leg bent.

4 Thrust right leg out to the side while pivoting. Strike with heel jutting outward.

5 Retract foot, bringing knee back to belt level and ready to strike out again.

94

Yoko geri
(from kiba dachi)

IN MOTION

1 Kiba dachi.

2 Cross right foot in front of the left, both heels lifted and legs bent. Pelvis remains level.

3 Raise and bend left knee at belt level, toes curled up.

4 Thrust left leg out to the side while pivoting on the right. Strike with the heel jutting outward.

5 Retract foot, bringing the knee back to belt level.

95

Yoko geri (from zen kutsu stance)

IN MOTION

1 Zen kutsu dachi.

2 Raise left knee to belt level, toes curled up.

3 Pivot on right foot, left leg bent.

4 Thrust left leg out while pivoting on the right foot. Strike with heel jutting outward.

5 Retract foot, bringing the knee back to the belt, ready to strike out again.

Ushiro geri
(BACK KICK)

IN MOTION

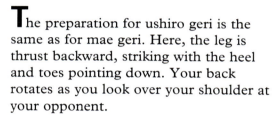

1 Zen kutsu dachi, left leg.

The preparation for ushiro geri is the same as for mae geri. Here, the leg is thrust backward, striking with the heel and toes pointing down. Your back rotates as you look over your shoulder at your opponent.

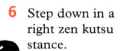

6 Step down in a right zen kutsu stance.

2 Start pivoting with the pelvis pushing backwards and legs bent.

5 Start pivoting forward.

3 Complete the rotation while raising right knee to belt level with toes curled up. Look over your shoulder at the opponent behind you.

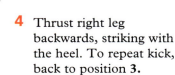

4 Thrust right leg backwards, striking with the heel. To repeat kick, back to position **3**.

Ippon kumite

(ONE-STEP SPARRING)

This exercise combines gohon and sambon kumite into a single attack. It is executed with the same spirit and with the same efficiency: speed, power, precision and determination.

Jyu ippon kumite

(SEMI-FREE ONE-STEP SPARRING)

This exercise, like ippon kumite, consists of a single attack but its purpose is different. It is similar to unlimited soft fighting in that both partners are mobile. Sparring begins in fudo dachi (immovable stance). Techniques and target areas are always prearranged. The attacker moves about freely waiting for an opportunity to strike.

THE KATAS

Heian sandan kata

Heian sandan is the third kata in the series. It introduces the use of kiba dachi.

THE KATAS
Heian sandan

▶ same position, front view

▶ same position, front view

▶ same position, front view

▶ same position, front view

▶ same position, front view

▶ same position, front view

▶ same position, front view

▶ same position, front view

▶ same position, front view

▶ same position, front view

▶ same position, front view

Blue Belt

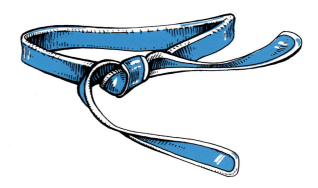

Congratulations! A green belt means you have made it through the hardest part. Now is not the time to let your training lapse. The blue belt program is relatively easy. However, you will start practising a new style of soft sparring called jyu kumite, which you may find challenging at first but surely exhilarating.

The techniques
TSUKI WASA
Koken
Age tsuki
Ura tsuki
KERI WASA
Mae hiza geri
Mawashi hiza geri
Ura mawashi
THE KATAS
Heian yodan

Tsuki Wasa

Koken

Koken can be used to block (uke) by striking upwards with the back of the wrist, fingers together and pointing down. Koken can also be used to attack (uchi) by delivering a strike from the side.

1 Kakuto or koken (strike with wrist in an upward motion).

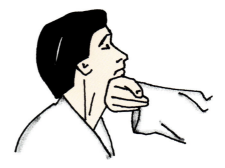

2 Kakuto or koken (strike with wrist from the side).

Age tsuki

3 Age tsuki (strike with back of fist in an upward motion). The punch starts below the target and curves upwards until it reaches its destination.

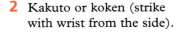

Ura tsuki (UPWARD CLOSE-IN PUNCH)

Ura tsuki is a technique used for close range attacks. The fingers are always facing up. It is an upward thrust which can be executed at three levels: gedan, shodan, or jodan.

IN MOTION

1 Hachigi dachi. Left arm extended and right fist at the hip.

3 Move into middle position. Hips at a 45° angle. Start striking cut with left fist while retracting right fist. Shoulders down.

2 Move left leg forward into zen kutsu. Strike upward with the right fist, palm facing up. Keep elbows close to the body. Arms bent at a 90° angle. Left fist at the hip.

4 Complete right zen kutsu stance. Strike upward with your left fist. Draw right fist back to the hip. Hips facing forward.

Keri Wasa

Mae hiza geri (KNEE KICK)

Mae hiza geri is a direct knee attack which can be executed at all three levels with or without grab. The preparation is the same as for mae geri but it is a close range technique.

1 Left zen kutsu stance. Both arms extended down to the sides for balance.

2 Thrust left knee upward keeping heel close to the thigh.

Mawashi hiza geri (ROUNDHOUSE KNEE KICK)

The knee kick can also be delivered in a semicircular motion as in mawashi geri. The knee and the foot are level, and the body pivots on the supporting leg.

1 Left zen kutsu stance. Both arms extended down to the sides for balance.

2 Raise knee to the side and strike in a circular motion, keeping the heel close to the thigh.

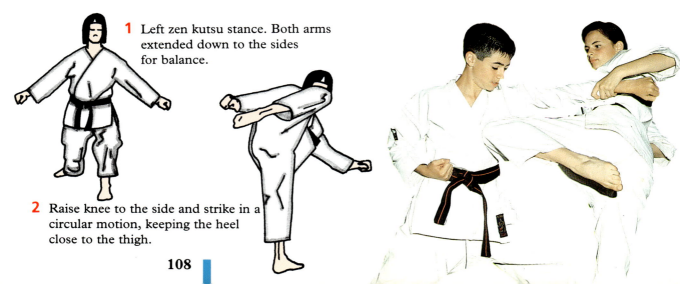

Ura mawashi
(REVERSE ROUNDHOUSE KICK)

In this technique, the leg sweeps around in a circular motion in the opposite direction of mawashi geri and strikes with the heel or the arch of the foot. Unlike ushiro geri, the kicking leg is bent.

IN MOTION

1 Right zen kutsu stance.

2 Raise left knee to the belt, toes curled up. Right leg bent.

3 Pivot on the right foot 90° clockwise. Shoulders down.

5 Sweep left leg around in a circular motion. Foot extended.

6 Bring foot back to buttocks. Body upright.

4 Pivot on the right foot 180° clockwise. Left foot level with the knee.

7 Back to position **2**.

8 Complete left zen kutsu stance.

Jyu kumite (FREE SPARRING) ▼▼▼▼▼▼▼▼▼▼▼▼

Gohon, sambon, ippon, and jyu ippon kumite have prepared you for free sparring. This is a soft type of training in which there are no restrictions save to avoid physical contact with the opponent. It is a fascinating game but also a difficult exercise in which you will have to apply with accuracy all the karate techniques you have learned.

APPLICATION

Heian yodan kata

Heian yodan, the fourth kata in the series, combines a large variety of techniques in a very interesting sequence.

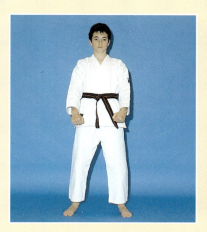

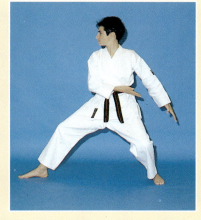

THE KATAS
Heian yodan

▶ same position, front view

▶ same position, front view

▶ same position, front view

THE KATAS
Heian yodan

▶same position, front view

116

Brown and Black Belts

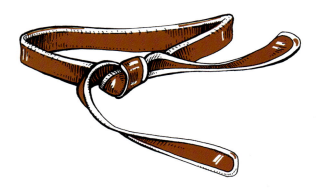

If you've been awarded your blue belt, congratulations! You are now ready to go on with your training for the highest rankings, the brown and black belts.

In this last program you will learn several new techniques, but most of your effort will be devoted to perfecting all the techniques learned so far. You will be practising your katas and kumites again and again. Basic techniques and kicks (kion) will be repeated during each training session. To obtain your brown and black belts, you must demonstrate in-motion mastery of all techniques, alone and with a partner.

The techniques
DACHI
Hangestsu dachi
TSUKI WASA
Tobikonde oi tsuki
Mawashi tsuki
Morote tsuki
Yama tsuki
Kagi tsuki
Teisho uchi
TSUKI WASA AND UKE WASA
Haito uchi and uke
KERI WASA
Fumikomi
Ushiro ura mawashi
THE KATAS

Dachi

Hangetsu dachi
(variation on kiba dachi)

This variation on the kiba dachi has both feet and knees pointing inward.

1 Same stance as kiba dachi except that toes and knees point inward.

Tsuki Wasa

Tobikonde oi tsuki

(JUMPING LUNGE PUNCH)

Tobikonde oi tsuki is a jumping lunge punch designed to close the distance between the attacker and the opponent if the latter is out of range or steps back.

1 Left zen kutsu stance.

2 Raise right knee and slide forward slightly on supporting leg, ready to lunge forward.

3 Step down into a right zen kutsu stance and attack with oi tsuki. Hips facing forward.

119

Mawashi tsuki (ROUNDHOUSE PUNCH)

This technique is executed by swinging the elbow out to the side and thrusting the fist forward in a circular motion. The elbow is slightly bent and the palm is facing downwards upon impact.

IN MOTION

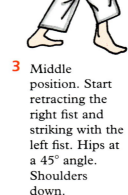

1 Hachigi dachi. Left arm extended and right fist at the hip.

2 Move left leg forward into zen kutsu. Punch out with the right fist in a circular motion while drawing the left fist back to the hip. Hips facing forward.

3 Middle position. Start retracting the right fist and striking with the left fist. Hips at a 45° angle. Shoulders down.

4 Complete right zen kutsu stance and punch with the left fist in a circular motion. Draw right fist back to the hip. Hips facing forward.

FRONT VIEW

1 Hachigi dachi. Left arm extended and right fist at the hip.

2 Move into a left zen kutsu stance. Punch with the right fist in a circular inward motion.

Morote tsuki (TWO-HAND PARALLEL PUNCH)

Morote tsuki is a two-hand punch which combines both oi tsuki and gyaku tsuki techniques. It can be aimed at all three levels.

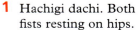

1 Hachigi dachi. Both fists resting on hips.

2 Kiba dachi. Punch out with both fists simultaneously, keeping elbows close to the body.

Yama tsuki (U-PUNCH)

This technique is similar to morote tsuki except that the arms are thrust out, one above the other, on two different levels. The upper fist can be used to block.

2 Move into a left zen kutsu stance and punch to target the face and the abdomen simultaneously, using both fists. Hips at a 45° angle.

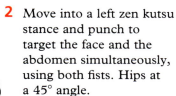

1 Hachigi dachi. Both fists at the right hip.

Kagi tsuki (HOOK PUNCH)

This is a close range technique directed at the opponent's side.

IN MOTION

1 Hachigi dachi. Left arm extended and right fist at the hip.

2 Kiba dachi. Bring right fist to the hip and left fist in front of body with arm slightly bent. Shoulders down.

3 Stationary: hook right-hand punch across the body and draw left fist back to the hip.

4 Move into kiba dachi while assuming ready position as in step 2. Pelvis remains level.

5 Complete kiba dachi and strike as in step 3.

Teisho uchi (PALM-HEEL STRIKE)

Teisho uchi is a versatile open-hand technique used to strike and to block. The heel of the palm is used as a striking surface.

IN MOTION

1 Hachigi dachi. Left arm extended and right fist at the hip.

2 Move left leg forward into zen kutsu. Strike with palm facing forward keeping elbows close to the body. Draw your left fist back to the hip. Hips facing forward.

3 Move into middle position. Hips at a 45° angle. Start striking out with the left arm and retracting the right fist to the hip. Shoulders down.

4 Complete right zen kutsu stance and left palm-heel strike.

123

Tsuki Wasa and Uke Wasa

Haito uchi and uke

(RIDGEHAND STRIKE AND BLOCK)

The inside edge of the open hand (from the base of the index finger to the folded thumb) is used for striking and for blocking. These techniques can be executed inward or outward.

IN PLACE

1 Hachigi dachi. Ready position with right hand under left arm, palm facing down and left arm extended. Shoulders down.

2 Rotate hips at a 45° angle. Right arm slides under left arm.

3 Complete hip rotation. Strike with the open hand, palm facing in, arm bent at a 90° angle. Left fist at the hip.

124

IN MOTION

6 Move into middle position. Hips facing forward. Left hand under right arm extended. Pelvis remains level.

5 Step forward with the right leg. Strike with the right hand and retract the left fist to the hip. Hips at a 45° angle. Shoulders down.

4 Hachigi dachi. Ready position as in step 1, stationary.

7 Complete left zen kutsu stance. Strike with the left hand, palm facing in. Right fist at the hip. Hips at a 45° angle.

Striking option

125

Keri Wasa

Fumikomi (STAMPING KICK)

This kick requires good preparation. The knee should be raised up high in order to increase the impact. This technique is a yoko geri at the gedan level and can be aimed at the foot, at the shin, or at the knee.

3 Pivot on supporting leg.

1 Right zen kutsu stance.

2 Bring knee up to the belt. Hips facing forward.

4 Thrust leg downwards while pivoting once again in order to pull the leg out from the hip. Strike with the outside edge of the foot.

5 Back to step 3.

6 Step down in a left zen kutsu stance.

Ushiro ura mawashi
(REAR ROTATING ROUNDHOUSE KICK)

This is a ura mawashi geri with a rotation completely towards the rear. Both the preparation and the movement remain the same.

IN MOTION

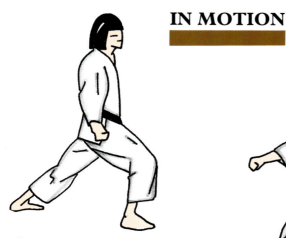

1 Right zen kutsu stance.

2 Use hips and supporting leg to pivot backwards. Head facing the opponent.

3 Raise left knee and foot to the belt. Shoulders down. Pelvis remains level.

4 Thrust left leg out and around with foot extended.

5 Bring left foot back to the buttocks keeping the body upright.

128

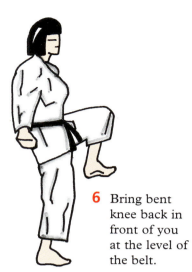

6 Bring bent knee back in front of you at the level of the belt.

7 Step down in a left zen kutsu stance.

Heian godan kata

Heian godan is the last basic kata in the series. It is a synthesis of the first four. Heian shodan, nidan, sandan, and yodan must be mastered before you start working on heian godan.

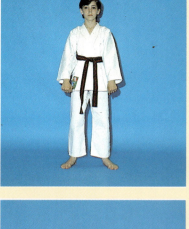

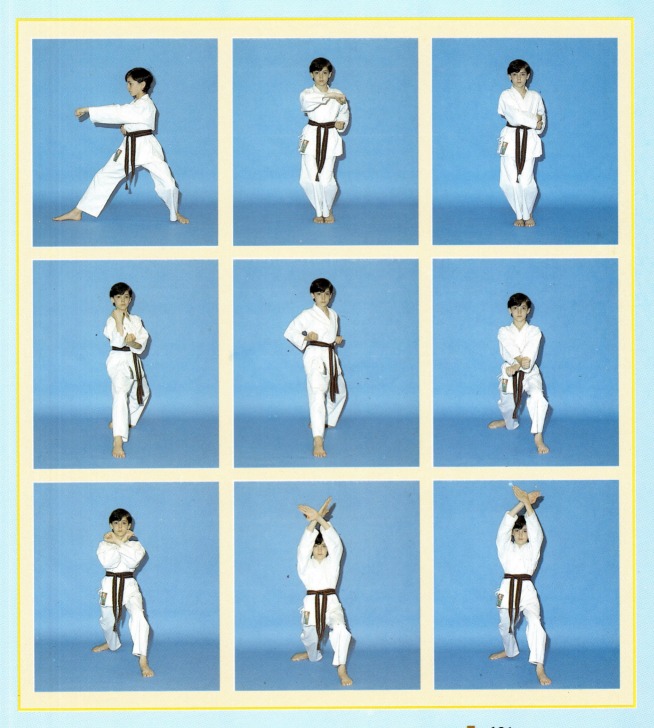

▶same position, front view   ▶same position, in profile

▶ same position, in profile

▶ same position, in profile

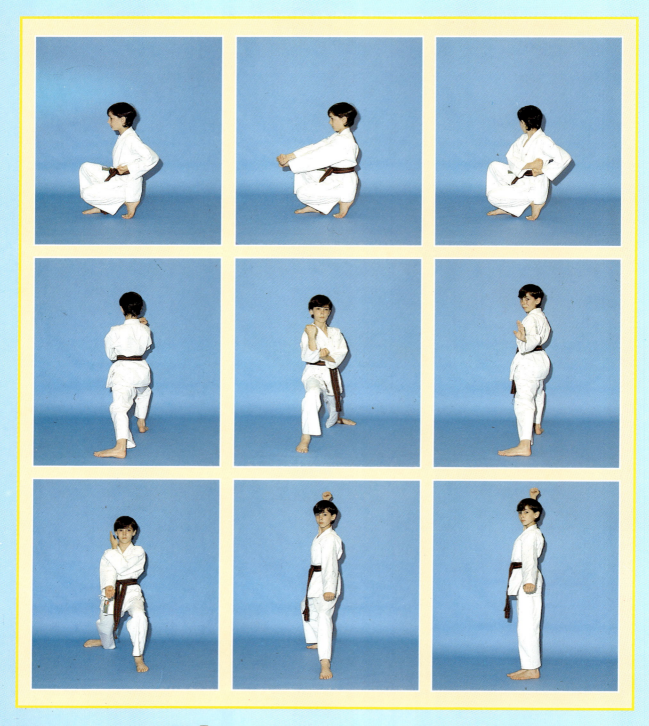

THE KATAS
Heian godan

IMPORTANT
This book presents only
the basic katas. You will
learn the others needed
for advancement in rank
with your instructor.

Competition

Competition is not mandatory, but taking part in it will enable you to acquire a greater mastery in the practice of karate. There are two types of competition: sparring and form (katas). Sparring with different opponents is important to developing good hand-eye coordination, correct breathing, sharpened reflexes, and personality. Competition gives you an opportunity to apply, within an unpredictable situation, all the techniques you have learned in the dojo. Using good sportsmanship while confronting an opponent will reinforce your sense of identity.

Technical competition is different from sparring. There is no opponent to contend with. You move alone within a given space, relying on total concentration and proper technique to execute your kata successfully. As you perform your kata before the judges and spectators, you will experience feelings that cannot really be shared with anyone. This experience will enrich you on an inner level. The two types of competition complement one another. By taking part in them, you will gain self-confidence and many other personal rewards.

Levels of competition

Competition may be available on several levels:
- Club or school competition (arranged by instructors or school officials)
- Local or regional competition (semiofficial)

In some parts of the world, there may also, from time to time, be official league, national, and world competitions scheduled. However, because of the numerous karate styles, or schools, with differing standards and rules, and not one "official" world organization, we will likely never see karate in the Olympics.

Requirements for entering competitions may vary, but often include a recent medical certificate and parental authorization for minors.

The schools or organizers will set age and rank (beginner, intermediate, or advanced) categories for competitions and provide instructions and rules for applicants. Depending on the number of participants, and the level of the competition, women and men usually compete separately. In addition to age, rank, and gender divisions, competitors may be further separated by weight classification, such as flyweight, lightweight, light-middleweight, middleweight, light-heavyweight, heavyweight.

What takes place at a kumite competition?

Sparring matches are held on a flat surface about 20 feet (6 meters) square. Strips of tape may mark the starting position of each contestant in the center of the contest area. Often, a total of five people are present to oversee and control the match, including three referees. Points and penalties are usually displayed on a panel nearby. Contestants are required to wear hand pads and a groin protector (men) or a chest protector (women). Other protective devices may be worn with medical approval.

Championship competition is divided up according to weight categories. These weight categories do not apply when competing for a cup. Contestants are paired off by random drawing.

Referee's signals during the match

Heikoku: Warning with wasa ari to the opponent (half-point penalty).

Jogai keikoku and **mubobi keikoku:** Referee points at feet of violator.

Jogai: Out of bounds.

Tsusukete: Get ready.

Hajime: Resume fighting, begin.

Wasa ari: A half-point awarded. Referee extends arm towards winner of award.

Hansoku chui: Warning with ippon to the opponent (one point penalty).

Jogai hansoku chui and **mubobi hansoku chui:** Referee points to abdomen of violator.

Yame: Stop, interruption, or end of match. Referee's hand cuts downward through the air.

Long technique

Technique lacking

Hikiwake: Draw. Referee crosses arms over chest, then lowers hands, palms forward.

Torimassen:
Unacceptable technique.
Referee crosses arms
over chest, then lowers
hands, palms down.

Technique or action
prohibited.

Ippon: One point or **no
kachi:** Referee raises
arm diagonally towards
side of winner.

Attack blocked.

Short technique

Shobu sambon hajime
and **shobu hajime:**
Start of match and
beginning of overtime.

Error in technique.

Aiuchi: Simultaneous
attack.

Hansoku or **shikkaku:**
Referee points to
violator and declares
opponent victor.

Keikoku or **mubobi:**
Warning or safety
violation.

Contact: Excessive
contact.

What takes place at a kata competition?

Although there are no set dimensions prescribed for the contest area, it must be large enough to allow contestants to execute their katas without being obstructed. The contestant enters the match area, faces the chief judge, bows, and announces the kata to be performed.

Kata competition generally takes place in three rounds. The order in which contestants perform is determined prior to each round.

Corner judges: **1, 2, 3, 4**
Chief judge: **5**
Contestant: **C**

The chief judge signals the corner judges to prepare to display their scores by blowing a whistle once. When the whistle is blown a second time, the corner judges hold up their scorecards.

Usually, a panel of five judges is appointed by the committee. Four judges are positioned at the corners of the match area while the fifth (chief) judge faces the contestant.

Kata championships are open to all age categories (from children to adults, men and women).

Introduction to junior competition (katas and sparring)

Competitions designed specifically for youngsters may be sponsored by private organizations or federal authorities on a regional level, so may apply only to certain age categories. Such competitions give children the chance to practise karate fully and help them grasp the true meaning of karate-do.

What happens at a junior competition?

In the first two rounds, both contestants are often required to perform the same kata simultaneously. The winner of the kata contest is given a bonus point (*ippon*). Sparring follows in the next round and lasts one minute. Helmets, hand pads, and groin or breast protectors are mandatory. Girls and boys compete separately.

Preparing for a junior competition

Master Gichin Funakoshi

The Origins of Karate

The discipline that is karate was introduced to China back in the sixth century by an Indian monk named Bodhidharma, who was believed to possess extraordinary powers. Noticing many of his disciples growing thin and weak from the rigors of an ascetic life, he taught them to control their bodies through breathing and limbering movements. It is said that he taught at a monastery called Shaolin, in northern China, that became a center for over four hundred styles of Chinese boxing, which originally used very slow and gentle movements.

Like many other Japanese masters, Gichin Funakoshi held his Chinese counterparts in profound admiration and respect. Born in

Okinawa in 1869, he demonstrated his technique for the first time in 1916 in Kyoto. A second demonstration took place in Tokyo in 1922 before a group of academics and the greatest martial art experts. It was such a success that he was invited to stay and teach his art. He opened a dojo in Tokyo and changed the name of the art from Okinawa-te to **"Karate-do"** (**kara,** empty; **te,** hand; and **do**, way; the suffix "do" stressing the significance of karate as a path leading to the unfolding of mind and body.

Karate-do was introduced to the United States in the 1950s and has been gaining in popularity ever since. Today, the discipline is world-renowned and practised by adults and children alike.

Index of Techniques